AN HOUR
OF
PRAYER

LENNOX MOSES

ARCHWAY
PUBLISHING

Archway Publishing books may be ordered
through booksellers or by contacting:

Archway Publishing
1663 Liberty Drive
Bloomington, IN 47403
www.archwaypublishing.com
844-669-3957

Scripture taken from the King James Version of the Bible.

ISBN: 978-1-6657-1641-3 (sc)
ISBN: 978-1-6657-1642-0 (e)

Library of Congress Control Number: 2022901214

Print information available on the last page.

Archway Publishing rev. date: 1/21/2022

PROLOGUE

Then He came to the disciples and found them sleeping, and He said to Peter:

"What, could you not watch with me ONE HOUR?"

"Watch and PRAY" [Matt 26: 40, 41]

So He left them and went away again, and prayed the THIRD time, saying THE SAME WORDS.
[Matt 26:44]

"I tell you, on the Day of Judgement, people will give account for every careless WORD they speak."

"For by your WORDS you will be justified, and by your WORDS you will be condemned."
[Matt 12:36-37]

"For whosoever shall call upon the NAME of the Lord, shall be saved." [Romans 10:13]

"I will set him on high because he knows my NAME. When he calls to me, I will answer him. I will be with him in trouble. I will deliver him and honor him. With long life will I satisfy him and show him my YESHUA" [Hebrew meaning: my Salvation] [Psalm 91:14-16]

Yeshua is Jesus's Hebrew name. It also means SALVATION. Jesus has many names. He is the Alpha and Omega, the Beginning and the End, the Son of God. He is called Wonderful, Counselor, Mighty God, Everlasting Father, the Prince of Peace. [Isaiah 9:6]

He is Yeshua Hamashiach, the Anointed One, the Messiah. This One Hour of Prayer uses all of these names, and many more. It is written to be read, but spoken, and is scheduled to last about an hour.

"What, could you not watch with me ONE HOUR?"

AN HOUR OF SPOKEN PRAYER

1

Hallelu-Yah, Hallelu-Yah, Hallelu-Yah. Praise the Everlasting, Almighty Creator God, who revealed his name to Moses as YHVH [Yod-He-Vav-He] meaning "Hand-revealed-Nail-revealed."

Elohei Yeshua-ti, El Yeshua-ti [God of my salvation]. Praise the everlasting Lord [El Olam] for his mercy endures forever. For you are holy, O You that inhabit the praises of Israel. [Psalm 22:3]

> Hear my prayer O Lord, give ear unto my supplications. In your faithfulness, answer me, and in your righteousness; and enter not into Judgement with

your servant .... for in your sight shall no man living be justified. [Psalm 143:2]

And Lord God, "Let the words of my mouth and the meditation of my heart be acceptable in your sight, O Lord, you are my Strength and my Redeemer." [Psalm 19:14]

Thank you, Jesus [Yeshua], for your grace, your mercy, and your blessings toward me. Emmanuel.

2

Father, hallowed be thy name. My Creator, I come to you in the name of your only begotten Son, my Lord and Savior, Lord Jesus Christ. Jesus Christ of Nazareth, you are called faithful and true, the High Priest forever, Wonderful, Counselor, mighty God, everlasting Father, the Prince of Peace, the Word of God, the Logos, Jesus Christ, the King of kings and Lord of lords, Emmanuel, the Elect One, the Holy One of God [John 6:69], the Promised Messiah, and the Anointed One.

Awesome God, El Gebhor [the Warrior God], El Shaddai, the Almighty God who created me, the Holy One of Israel, the King of Glory, Ha' Elyon [the Most High], I bless and magnify your name. I worship you,

YHVH Shammah [the Lord is there], Yahweh, Lord God. I give you glory, honor, and praise. I sing praises to you, Lord God.

> Holy, Holy, Holy,
> Lord God Almighty,
> Early in the Morning,
> my song shall rise to thee.
>
> Holy, holy, holy,
> All the saints adore thee,
> casting down their golden crowns
> around the glassy sea.
>
> Cherubim and seraphim,
> falling down before thee,
> who wert, and art,
> and evermore shalt be.[1]

Your name, Jesus, Yeshua, is above all names. Cover me with your name. Cover me with the blood of Jesus Christ, the blood of Yeshua Hamashiach [the Anointed One]. "Holy, Holy, Holy, is the Lord of Hosts, the whole earth is full of his glory," as the angels say in Isaiah 6:3.

---

[1] Lyrics by Reginald Heber.

Lord God Almighty, Lord of Glory, Creator of heaven and earth, you are worthy to be praised, O Lord, and to be "high and lifted up," [Isaiah 6:1] glorified, and magnified forever. Thank you, Jesus, Yeshua, for all you have done for me.

Spirit of God, Holy Spirit, Spirit of the Most High, Spirit of the Living God, breathe in me. O Holy Spirit, pray to the Almighty Father. Spirit, pray through me, teach me how to pray and what things to pray for. Lord Jesus, you are the fountain, the river, the stream of Living Water. The Spirit, the Water, and the Blood bear witness in the blood and in the mighty name of the Lord Jesus Christ of Nazareth.

Abba, Father, merciful and gracious Father, remember me. I pray, in the mighty name of Jesus, Son of David, have mercy on me. I am not worthy, Lord God, Lord Jesus Christ. I know that I am undeserving of your mercy. Find me in your mercy, O Lord, find me in your favor. Let your mercy find me, O Lord. Let your favor find me, in the name of Jesus Christ, in the name of Yeshua Hamashiach.

3

———

"Our Father which art in heaven, hallowed be thy name, thy kingdom come, thy will be done on earth, as it is in heaven. Give us this day our daily bread. And forgive us our trespasses as we forgive those that trespass against us. And lead us not into temptation but deliver us from evil. For thine is the kingdom, and the power and the glory, forever and ever" [Matthew 6:9–13]. In the mighty name of Jesus Christ, Yeshua Hamashiach [the Anointed One], I pray.

Father God, I CONFESS all my sins before you, O Lord. I REPENT of all my sins, O Lord. Forgive me for breaking any of your Ten Commandments. Father, forgive all my sins, iniquities, and transgressions—those known or unknown, those of omission or commission, and those committed consciously or unconsciously by thought, word, or deed—and help me to forgive those who have trespassed against me. Lord God, remember my sins no more, and lead me not into temptation. "Have mercy upon me, O God, according to your loving kindness, according unto the multitude of your tender mercies, blot out all my transgressions. Wash me thoroughly from all mine iniquities and cleanse me from all my sins, make them as white as snow." [Psalm 51:1–2]

Father, Lord Jesus Christ, Yeshua Hamashiach, it is against you that I have sinned. Forgive me all my sins, O Lord, and cleanse me of all unrighteousness. Break the power of sin over me. Help me to forgive all those who have offended me. Lord, Son of David, have mercy on me. Cleanse me, O Father, of all unrighteousness by the precious blood of the Lamb of God, who was slain on the Cross of Calvary for my sins. "Create in me a clean heart and renew a right spirit within me" [Psalm 51:10]. Deliver me from the spirit of anger. Thank you for hearing the prayers of anyone, made on my behalf, and for your extreme mercy and grace toward me, O God.

In my spirit, Lord, let there be no guile. Deliver me from the spirit of offense, from Unforgiveness, from pain of the past, and from any grudges or envy. Deliver me from the lusts of the flesh, from the lusts of the eyes, and from the pride of life. Grant me the fear of the Lord, the mind of Christ, and the wisdom, patience, and understanding that you give to those who seek these blessings. Bless me with your Holy Spirit, bless me in all my activities, and guide me. Grant me love, a hearing heart, and the fruits of the Spirit.

O Lord, order my steps in your Word. Let me know where I am missing the mark, and help me to live by your Word. Help me to walk blamelessly before you in thought, word, and deed. I pray that I be found worthy of, and grant me a place in, your eternal kingdom. Deliver me from any plagues or pandemics. Remember, Lord, your promise to those who call on your name:

> You shall not be afraid
> for the terror by night,
> nor for the arrow that flies
> by day.

Nor for the pestilence that walks
in darkness,
nor for the destruction that wastes
at noonday.

A thousand shall fall at your side,
ten thousand at your right hand,
but it shall not come near you.
[Psalm 91:5–7]

4

Let me be baptized with your Holy Spirit, Lord Jesus. Let my words, thoughts, and actions reflect you, in the mighty name of my Lord and Savior Jesus Christ. In the name, and the holy and righteous blood of Yeshua Hamashiach of Nazareth I pray. Thank you, Father; thank you, Jesus Christ, Yeshua Hamashiach, thank You, Holy Spirit.

O Lord, my God, O Ancient of Days, God of Abraham, God of Isaac, God of Jacob, grant to me your mercy and my heart's desires, favor, and grace. Answer my prayers, O Lord. My Lord and Savior, Lord Jesus Christ, you said in Matthew 7:7, "Ask, and it will be given to you."

In John 14:13, you promised, "Whatsoever you ask the Father, in my name, that will I do."

Abba, Father, in the Mighty Name of the Lord and Savior Jesus Christ of Nazareth, in the name of Yeshua Hamashiach, grant me the gift of Eternal Life, bless my family, grant them your salvation, grant them the gift of Eternal Life, and save and bless them in every possible way. Cover my family with your precious blood, in the mighty name of my Lord and Savior Jesus Christ of Nazareth, in the blood and name of Yeshua Hamashiach of Nazareth.

Lord Jesus, Yeshua, you are the only one in our world who was crucified for the sins of mankind, was hung on the Cross for our iniquities, and only by your shed blood could we be redeemed, and be given the gift of Eternal Life. As you said in your Word: "Whoever drinks the water I shall give them, will never thirst. Indeed, the water I give them will become in them a spring of water, welling up to Eternal Life." [John 4:14 NIV]

O Lord, let us say, like the woman of Samaria: "Sir, give me this water [to drink] that I never thirst."

[John 4:15]

And give me the Fear of the Lord, of which you say: "The Fear of the Lord is the beginning of Wisdom, and knowledge of the Holy One is Understanding."

[Proverbs 9:10]

Let me fear no man, but Fear only God. In your Word, you said: "Fear not those who can only kill the body, but cannot hurt the soul; rather fear Him which is able to destroy both soul and body in Gehenna" [hell].

[Matthew 10:28]

[Mace NT]

5

Almighty Father, O great I Am, I Am, I Was, and I Will Be; I Am That I Am; Yahovah; Yahweh; YAH [Psalm 68:4]; Abba Father, in the name of the Lord and Savior, Jesus Christ of Nazareth and in the name of Yeshua Msheekha [the Messiah], grant these prayers in the precious blood of my Lord and Savior, Jesus Christ of Nazareth, and in the mighty name of Yeshua Hamashiach of Nazareth. Yahovah Rapha [the Lord my Healer], you are our Healer, Lord, as You said in Isaiah 53:5.

> But He was wounded for OUR transgressions,
> He was bruised for our iniquities,

The chastisement of our peace was
upon Him,
And with his stripes we are healed.

"Heal me, O Lord, and I shall be healed, save me, and
I shall be saved, for thou art my praise."
[Jeremiah 17:14]

Also, O Lord, forgive me my desires to fulfil the lusts of
the flesh, for not all desires are good for me to pursue, as
"many foolish and harmful desires plunge people into
ruin and destruction."
[1 Timothy 6:9]

As it says in your Word, "Now the works of the flesh
are evident: sexual immorality, impurity, sensuality,
idolatry, sorcery, enmity, strife, jealousy, fits of anger,
rivalries, dissentions, divisions, envy, drunkenness,
orgies and things like these. I warn you, as I warned
you before, that those who do such things will not
inherit the kingdom of God." [Galatians 5:19-21 ESV]

Lord Jesus, deliver us from offense and let us confess
our sins before you and repent of our sins. Forgive me
my sins, O Lord. Let the blood of Jesus cover me, and

Lord God, heal and cover us with your stripes and with the blood of Jesus Christ and in the mighty name of Yeshua Hamashiach of Nazareth. Jeremiah 29:11 says, "For I know the plans I have for you, declares the Lord, plans to prosper you and not harm you, plans to give you hope and a future."

Father of all, Father of Lights, Most High Yah. "Let there be light" in me and in every area of my life in Jesus's name. Jesus, you are the light of the world. You are my Helper. God who answers by fire, Yahovah Tsidkenu [the Lord our Righteousness], Yahovah Sabaoth [the Lord of Hosts], reverse every curse made against me, in the name of Yeshua Hamashiach.

To you, any enemies, human or spiritual, who want my downfall, the Lord my God will fight for me. May the Lord rebuke you, in the Mighty Name of the Lord Jesus Christ and by the Blood and Name of Yeshua Hamashiach.

6

―――――

Lord of Spirits, I bind every spirit not of God operating anywhere in me, or around me, in my given name .... in my life, and in whatever concerns me, "Whatever you bind on earth, shall be bound in heaven. Whatever you loose on earth, shall be loosed in heaven." [Matthew 16:19]

I bind their kings with chains and their nobles with fetters of iron. I execute upon them the judgments written. This honor have all his saints" as it says in Ps 149:8.

I have this honor. I command/I loose Holy Ghost Fire on any evil forces, on any unclean, any familiar, any contrary, any generational spirits, or any evil ancestral spirits or evil demons, idols and false gods operating against me. I send ANY evil thoughts or plans from any human beings or demons back to sender.

I give honor to my father and mother, and Lord God, help them to forgive me any transgressions that I may have committed against them, and Lord God, help me to forgive them all transgressions they may have committed against me, and I pray that they be counted worthy to be in your Eternal kingdom, Lord, and to all my other ancestors, I embrace you all and all of your good hopes and dreams of success for your seed, for me and my family.

You principalities, you powers, you liars, you thieves that only come to kill, steal and destroy, you any spirits not of God, Out, Out, Out of my life and never return in the Mighty Name of Jesus Christ, the name Yeshua Hamashiach.
In Deuteronomy 28:13 it is written, "YHVH will make me the head and not the tail, that I shall be above only and that I shall not be beneath."

In Proverbs 13:21 it is written: "the righteous shall be rewarded with Prosperity."

Give me the Fear of the Lord, Give me Truth, Wisdom and Understanding, Lord, which you say you give freely to those that ask.

In Prov 16:3 it says: "Commit whatever you do to the Lord, and your plans will succeed." All success doors that are closed: Be opened now in the Mighty Name of Jesus Christ, in the name of Yeshua Hamashiach.

I command, I decree, that everything that you evil spirits have stolen from me, my star, my crown, my destiny, my shalom peace, my blessings, my money, my assets, anything of value that you enemies human or spiritual, have stolen from me, I command them to be returned now from the north, south, east and west and from wherever they are, and to be restored to me in the Name of my Lord and Savior, Jesus Christ, and the Blood of Jesus Christ, Yeshua Hamashiach.

7

Heavenly Father, whose name is written as Y-H-V-H, Lord of Glory, in the Mighty Name of my Lord and Savior Jesus Christ of Nazareth, Yeshua Hamashiach, I ask that the name of Yeshua Hamashiach and the precious Blood of Jesus Christ, cover me, cover my family, heal them and bless them. O Lord God, the name of Jesus Christ, the precious Blood of Yeshua Hamashiach, cover their names, bless them, Lord, with Mercy, Grace, and Favor, forgive them all their sins, O Lord God, and protect them. Peace be unto them.

In your infinite mercy, O Lord, deliver .... from any contrary, any familiar spirits, deliver them from Lucifer, from any demons, monitoring spirits, spiritual husband spirits in dreams, spiritual wife spirits in dreams, or any evil activities committed in dreams. Come out you unclean spirits, you marine spirits, you giant man and strongman spirits, and, O God, remove any evil influence from their names, and deliver them from any demons that try to delay or steal their destinies. Deliver them from evil, and from the evil One in the Mighty Name of the Lord & Savior Jesus Christ of Nazareth, in the blood and name of Yeshua Hamashiach.

You the evil One, may the Lord God, whose name is written as YHVH, Elohei Yeshua-ti, El Yeshua-ti [God of my Salvation], Yahovah, Yahweh, YAH, Abba Father, may He rebuke you, the evil One, in the Mighty Name of Jesus Christ, Yeshua Hamashiach. You spiritual husband and spiritual wife spirits in dreams, you strongman spirits, you giant man spirits, you spiritual husband demons, you Lucifer, you any spirits not of God, whatever names you call yourselves, come out, come out, come out of me, and out of .... Fire from the Holy Ghost against you .... in the Mighty Name and the Blood of my Lord and Savior Jesus Christ of Nazareth, in the blood of Yeshua Hamashiach of Nazareth, whose blood was shed for our sins, shed for our sakes. Jesus, Yeshua is Lord.

You monitoring spirits, I call you by name. You Lucifer, come out, come out, come out of ...... and out of ......, you Spirit of Anger, you Spirit of Offense, you spirit of Pain of the Past, you spirit of Resentment, you spirit of Jealousy. Come out of .... you unclean spirits [Mark 5:8] you any spirits not of God, you marine spirits, you demons, that only come to kill, steal and destroy, whatever names you call yourselves, whatever names you are, come out of ...... in the blood of Jesus Christ, and in the Name of Yeshua Hamashiach of Nazareth I pray.

You any spirits not of God affecting ...., whatever names you call yourselves, "hear the Word of the Lord, I bind you all in chains and I send you back to the pit of hell from whence you came."

I send Holy Ghost Fire against you in the Mighty Name and blood of my Lord and Savior Jesus Christ of Nazareth. Fire in the Name of Jesus Christ, Fire in the name of Yeshua Hamashiach. Fire from the Holy Ghost. I command you - - Be cast out. Come out

from ......, come out from ...., and come out ......
from .... you unclean spirits, and never return
to them ...., be delivered now from all demons in
the Mighty Name of my Lord and Savior Jesus Christ
of Nazareth and by the righteous and holy blood and
name of Yeshua Hamashiach of Nazareth. Thank you
Jesus Christ.

8

Lord Jesus, in your mercy and in your grace, grant me and my family the gift of Eternal Life, I pray. I command Holy Ghost Fire on any spirits not of God affecting relationships with my family in the Name of Jesus Christ and in the Blood of Yeshua Hamashiach. [Isaiah 14:12]

Lord God, I thank you for blessing my house, for blessing my family and friends, for blessing my career, for blessing my health, blessing their health, and as written in Job 42:10 "And the Lord turned the captivity of Job when he had prayed for his friends." Bless my friends, O Lord. Hear my prayer for my companions and bless their lives.

In the name of Jesus Christ, Yeshua Hamashiach, the name given by God above all names, that at the name of Jesus, Yeshua, every knee shall bow, of things in heaven, and things on earth, and things under the earth, and that every tongue shall confess that Jesus Christ, Yeshua Hamashiach is Lord, to the glory of God the Father." [Philippians 2:10]

"For there is One God, and One Mediator between God and men, the man Christ Jesus, who gave himself a ransom for all, to be testified in due time." [1 Timothy 2:5]

Your name, Jesus [Yeshua] is: "Far above all rule and authority, above principalities and powers, and dominion, and above every name that is invoked, not only in the present age, but also in the one to come. [Ephesians 1:21]. Praise the Lord, the Everlasting Father. Thank you my Lord and Savior Jesus Christ, Yeshua Hamashiach, thank you, Holy Spirit.

9

Yahovah Jireh, my Provider, you said in Proverbs 13:22 "a good man leaves an inheritance for his children's children." Make me a good man, Lord, my righteousness is of you, you are Yahovah Tsidkenu, the Lord our Righteousness. You said in [Genesis 22 verses16-17], "By myself have I sworn, saith the Lord, that surely in blessing I will bless you, and in multiplying I will multiply you," in Jesus Christ name, Yeshua Hamashiach.

Thank you for blessing and multiplying me, Lord, Everlasting God, covenant-keeping God, I claim the blessings of Abraham for myself as a son of Abraham by faith, and as in [Deuteronomy 8:18], I remember the

Lord my God, and I thank you, Lord, for it is you that is giving me the power to get wealth.

In [Matthew 7: 7] you said "Ask and it shall be given to you.' In [Luke 6:38], Jesus, you said that I shall receive "good measure, pressed down, shaken together and running over" in Jesus Christ, Yeshua Hamashiach's name.

As you said in Joel 2:23-26, I thank you, Almighty God for your PROMISE to "restore to me the years that the locusts have eaten, and the cankerworm, and the caterpillar and the palmerworm, your great army that you sent to me." Bless my finances, bless my work, and thank you for my job, in the Name of Jesus Christ, I pray.

Thank you for "rebuking the devourer for my sake" as you said in [Malachi 3:11], thank you for raining on me, for restoring my lost years, for letting me eat in plenty and be satisfied and praise the name of the Lord, my God, that has dealt wonderously with me," in the name of Jesus, Yeshua, I pray. Lord, you said in Psalm 112:3 that "Wealth and riches shall be in my house, and that my righteousness shall endure forever."

Lord, indeed as it is written in Psalm 113:7, "You raise the poor out of the dust, and lift the needy, out of the dunghill." "Whatever I bind on earth, shall be bound in heaven, whatever I loose on earth, shall be loosed in heaven. [Matthew 18:19]. I am successful. I loose success in all my endeavors, in Jesus Christ, Yeshua Hamashiach's name.

In Proverbs you said: "The blessing of the Lord it maketh rich, and He adds no sorrow with it."
[Proverbs 10:22]
Lord Jesus, you have said "I have come that you might have life and have it more abundantly."
[John 10:10]
O Lord, my Father, my Helper, I ask in the name of Jesus Christ and in the blood of Jesus, shed for us, the blood of Yeshua Hamashiach, that you provide my help, and provide for me my heart's desires, provide that more abundant life, ..., a ...., and ...., and bless my finances, O Lord, in the Mighty name of Jesus, Yeshua Hamashiach.

As it is written in Joshua 1:3. "Every place that the sole of thy foot shall tread upon, that have I given unto you, as I said unto Moses." In the blood of Jesus Christ and in the Name of the Lord Yeshua Hamashiach of Nazareth I pray. Bless my assets in the name of Jesus, Yeshua, Lord, the Everlasting God.

As it is written, "and the Spirit of God moved upon the face of the waters, and God said: Let there be light," and there was light." Spirit of God, move upon the face of the waters. "Let there be light" in all my finances, in all my assets, and there was light, in all my finances, in all my assets in Jesus's name, in the name and blood of Yeshua Hamashiach.

"You my assets, you my money, you my financial assets "Be fruitful and multiply" in Jesus Christ, Yeshua Hamashiach's name. Abba, Father, grant this prayer which I pray in the Blood and in the name of my Lord and Savior Jesus Christ, Yeshua Hamashiach of Nazareth.

10

Yahovah Raah [The Lord my Shepherd] Adonai [The Lord My Master] El Gibbor [Great and Mighty God] Yahovah Nissi [The Lord my Banner] Yahovah Shalom [The Lord my Peace] Eloheeka [The Lord my God], Father, the only True God and Jesus Christ who you have sent, O Father, Holy Father, Father, Father, O Righteous Father, deliver me from the evil one and from evil, as David says in the 27th Psalm:

> The Lord is my light and my salvation,
> whom shall I fear,
> the Lord is the strength of my life,
> of whom shall I be afraid,

When the wicked, even my enemies
and my foes,
came up upon me to eat up my flesh,
they stumbled and fell,

Though an host should encamp
against me,
my heart shall not fear,
though war should rise against me,
in this will I be confident."
[Psalm 27:1-3]

Cover me with your precious blood, and bless me in every area of my life in Jesus's name, Yeshua. My Redeemer, I loose every chain that the devil has used to tie me to himself, and to setback, to disappointment, to limitation and failure. Defeat, failure, disappointment and limitation are things of the past. Thank you for your mercy, O Lord. Thank you for your favor. Lord Jesus, you are the Root and the Offspring of David and the Bright and Morning Star [Revelation 22:16] You are the Bread of Life, the Light of the World, the Door, the True Vine, the Resurrection and the Life, the Promised Messiah.

In Psalm 149:4 you said "The Lord taketh pleasure in his people, He will beautify the meek with Salvation." Thank you Lord, for beautifying me with Salvation. "I will praise you for I am fearfully and wonderfully made, marvelous are thy works" [Psalm 139:14]. O Lord my Maker [Elohim Hoseenu], King of Kings and Lord of Lords, God of gods, manifest yourself in my life, and as in Psalm 103, "satisfy my years with good things, so that my youth is renewed like the eagles," in the Mighty Name of Jesus Christ, Yeshua Hamashiach.

Lord, you are the Son of King David of Israel who had made the ultimate plea to the Father of All as he prayed, "Search me, O God, and know my heart, try me, and know my thoughts, and see if there be any wicked way in me, and lead me in the Way Everlasting." [Psalm 139:23-24]

11

Jesus Christ, Yeshua Hamashiach, you are the Son of the Living God, you are the King of Shiloh, as prophesied back in Genesis:

> The sceptre shall not depart
> from Judah,
> nor a lawgiver from between his feet,
> until Shiloh come,
> and unto him shall the gathering of
> the people be." [Genesis 49:10]

You are the Head of the body, the Church, the Firstborn from the dead, Son of God, Son of Man, Son of the Most High, my Sanctifier, my Defender, the Prince of

Peace, the Soon Coming King, you are the Resurrection and the Life, the King of Love, the Good Shepherd, the Daystar and the Dayspring from on High, Jesus Christ of Nazareth, the Messiah, Rabboni, My Lord, my Great Master, Eternal God, Everlasting God, my Creator, the Creator of all, Ha'Elyon [the Most High] El Roi [the God who sees me] El Deot [the God of Knowledge] El Emet (the God of Truth] El Channun [the Gracious God]. Yahovah Mekadesh [the Lord who makes me holy] EL, Elie, Eloi, Elohim, Eloah, Elohai, Elie-Yah, YAH, "Leave me not neither forsake me, O God of my Salvation." [Psalm 27:9]

Thank you Jesus for your limitless mercy and your unbounded grace towards me. Y-H-V-H, YAH, "my refuge, my fortress, my Elohim in whom I trust," the Lord God of Gods, I believe in you. You said in Psalm 91:14-16:

> Because he hath set his love upon me,
> therefore will I deliver him.
> I will set him on high,
> because he knows my NAME.
>
> When he calls to me, I will answer him.

I will be with him in trouble.
I will deliver him and honor him.
With long life will I satisfy him,
and show him my YESHUA [Hebrew
meaning: my Salvation]

Yeshua, Jesus, you are Salvation, our Savior, the Messiah,
God as Savior. Father, you declared your name:

"I am YHVH that is my Name." [Isaiah 42:8]

YHVH, Lord God, you are a consuming fire, a jealous
God, as it says in your word: "For the Lord thy God is
a consuming fire, even a jealous God." [El Quanna] in
Deuteronomy 4:24, and Moses published your Name
in the Song of Moses:

"Give ear, O ye heavens
And I will speak, and hear O earth,
the words of my mouth,
My doctrine shall drop as the rain,
my speech shall distil as the dew.

As the small rain upon the tender herb,
and as the showers upon the grass,

because I will publish the name of

YHVH

ascribe ye greatness unto our God.

Deuteronomy 32: 1-3]

"YHVH, our Lord, how Majestic is your name in all the earth." [Psalm 8:9 NIV]

Eternal God, you described yourself to Moses as "Ehyeh Asher Ehyeh" meaning "I Am, I Am What I Am, I Will Be What I Will Be" [Exodus 3:14]

You became Savior, Salvation, through your Son, the Savior, the Lion of Judah, Yeshua Hamashiach, the Lord Jesus Christ of Nazareth. Lord God, my trust is in you, I KNOW that my Redeemer lives.

Thank you for answering my prayers which I pray, in the name of Jesus Christ, Yeshua Hamashiach, in the name of Jesus Christ, Yeshua Hamashiach, in the Mighty Name of Jesus Christ, Yeshua Hamashiach I pray.

12

Jesus Christ, the Name Jesus - - the Way, the Truth and the Life, the Alpha and Omega, the Beginning and the End, the Amen, the First and the Last, and the Blood of Jesus Christ, Yeshua Hamashiach of Nazareth. Emmanuel, the Word of God that was shed on the Cross, the Blood of Jesus who was crucified for us at Calvary, thank you Jesus.

Cover this prayer with the Blood of Jesus, Yeshua. Wash me clean by the precious Blood of the Lamb of God, and cover me with his blood. I thank you for healing my body, for healing my ...., and for covering everything that concerns me with the Blood of Jesus, in the name of Jesus Christ, in the Blood of

Yeshua Hamashiach I pray. Jesus, you are the Lion of Judah, my trust is in you. In your infinite mercy, O Lord, forgive me any additions, omissions and any mischaracterizations in this prayer.

Emmanuel, Jesus Christ, Yeshua Hamashiach. Halleluyah. Jesus, Yeshua is Lord. Thank you Jesus, you are the King of Mount Zion [the Mount of Peace] the city of the Living God. [Hebrews 12:22]

O Lord God Almighty, the consonants of whose name are written as: "Y-H-V-H, your name be praised." For thine is the kingdom, and the power, and the glory, forever and ever. Glory be to God in the highest. Blessed be your name, YHVH, Father I worship you.

I exault your Name. Blessed be your name, Yeshua Hamashiach, Our Savior, Lord God, forever and ever. Praise the Lord. Hallelujah, Elohei Yeshua-ti, El Yeshua-ti [God is my Salvation] Yeshua Msheekha [the Messiah] Yahovah, Yahweh, YAH, Abba, Father, in the Mighty Name of Jesus Christ and in the blood of the Lamb of God, the Lord of Glory, the Lord Yeshua Hamashiach of Nazareth, hear and answer these my prayers in the name of Yeshua Hamashiach, in the name of my Lord and Savior Jesus Christ of Nazareth and in the Blood of Jesus Christ, and cover this prayer with his precious blood.

"Worthy is the Lamb that was slain, to receive power, and riches and wisdom and strength and honor and glory and blessing." [Revelation 5:11-12]
For thine is the kingdom, and the power and the glory, forever and ever, in Jesus Christ of Nazareth's name, in the name of Yeshua Hamashiach of Nazareth I pray. Hosanna in the highest. Praise the Everlasting Lord. Praise the Everlasting Lord. Praise the Everlasting Lord! Amen and Amen.

EPILOGUE

Thanks to the Everlasting God, and to his Son Jesus Christ, Yeshua Hamashiach, who was crucified on the Cross for our sins, and to the Holy Spirit. I cannot thank you enough, Lord, for the honor you have given me to write this book of One Hour of Spoken Prayer.

My thanks also go out to Jeremiah, who was a 3 year old genius, when I first saw him on TV in 2020. His intellect at 3 years of age, left me truly amazed. It was his very short but deep and heartfelt prayer at the end of one of his sessions which inspires this very work.

Thanks also to my children, to my son, who I happily notice, naturally has some of my own instincts, and to my two young daughters, who have caused me to pray even more fervently over the last few years.

I hope that this one hour of spoken prayer will reach and inspire as many people as possible, in as many languages as possible, all over the world, and that people will use it to call on the NAME of the Lord.

Prayers, any prayers, made with sincerity, will produce changes in your life, and may perhaps be "a spring of water, welling up into Eternal Life." [John 4:14]

I believe that for many of us, it is difficult to pray for one hour, as we run out of things to pray for, and after a few minutes, we are hard-pressed to find something meaningful and significant to say. This Book of an Hour of Prayer helps solve that problem.

Lennox Moses
lm1129@hotmail.com

CPSIA information can be obtained
at www.ICGtesting.com
Printed in the USA
LVHW030624020322
712306LV00002B/377